Odd One Out

By John Satchwell
Illustrated by Katy Sleight

PUBLISHED BY
DISCOVERY TOYS

1 lonely monster

looking for
another monster.

1 monster

1 horse

1 monster

2 cows

1 monster

3 sheep

1 monster

4 pigs

1 monster

5 dogs

1 monster

6 cats

1 monster

7 rabbits

1 monster

8 hens

1 monster

9 ducks

1 monster

10 mice

2 monsters

How many monsters?